Short ish Walks
Lower Tamar Valley

Paul White

Bossiney Books

First published 2011 by
Bossiney Books Ltd, 33 Queens Drive, Ilkley, LS29 4QW
www.bossineybooks.com

ISBN 978-1-906474-34-8

Acknowledgements

The maps are by Graham Hallowell. All photographs are by the author.
Cover based on a design by Heards Design Partnership.
The boots on the front cover were kindly supplied by The Brasher Boot Company.

Printed in Great Britain by R Booth Ltd, Penryn, Cornwall

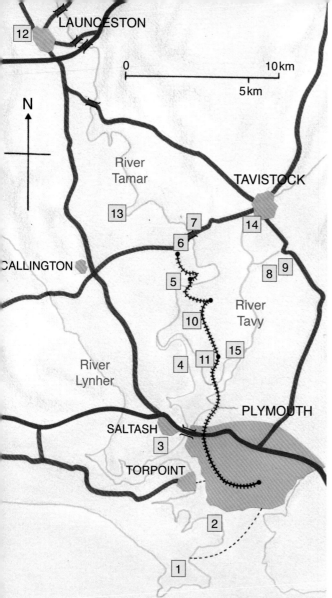

The approximate locations of the walks in this book.

Most are circular but Walks 13-15 are there-and-back walks.

Whilst the area around the navigable Tamar and its tributaries has footpaths and bridleways in profusion, north of Gunnislake they become fewer, and it is much harder to find appropriate walks.

In compensation, we have included one very different walk – more of a town trail – at Launceston, which is an ancient town of considerable interest.

For several of the walks, the ideal way to approach them is by the Tamar Valley railway line, an extraordinary survivor of the Beeching cuts which makes a great day out in its own right.

All the walks in this book were checked prior to publication, at which time the instructions were correct. However, changes can occur in the countryside over which neither the author nor the publisher has any control. Please let us know if you encounter any serious problems.

On many of these walks you will notice incongruous ivy-clad ruins, like this mine chimney on Walk 8

Introduction

The River Tamar used to be a vital commercial artery for the valley, with dozens of quays dotted along its shores and those of its major tributaries, the Tavy and the Lynher.

This made possible the growth of two major industries. Many of the south-facing slopes were once market gardens; and mining was important, especially in the early fourteenth century (for silver near Weir Quay) and the mid-nineteenth (for copper, north of Gunnislake).

All this activity required packhorse and cart tracks, many of which survive as footpaths and bridleways, even though their industries are long gone, leaving occasional ivy-clad ruins in the woods.

The 'shortish' walks in this book are mostly 6-8 km in length (4-5 miles) and can be completed in a couple of hours.

These are rural walks, and you should expect some mud. And after wet weather a lot of mud. Proper walking boots or shoes are essential. (Wellingtons are not recommended.) In summer there will be briars or nettles, so bare legs are a liability.

Do take a spare layer for extra warmth, as well as waterproofs. Drinking water is important, as dehydration causes tiredness.

We hope you won't get lost using our sketch maps, but you may well want to carry the OS Explorer map 108 which gives a lot more detail.

The countryside

Farmers are trying to make a living out of much of the countryside you pass through. Please respect their crops, leave gates closed or open as you find them, and keep dogs under control, especially during the lambing season.

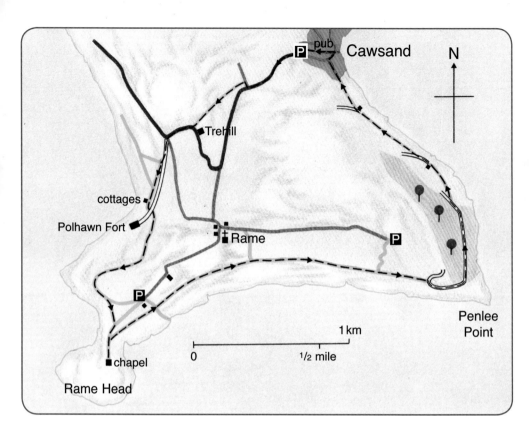

Walk 1   Rame Head from Cawsand

Distance: 7.6km (4³/4 miles)   Time: 2 hours
Character: Mainly a coast path walk round a headland, starting from
the fascinating village of Cawsand (and its twin village, Kingsand)
which can be reached by ferry (summer only) from Plymouth.
An alternative starting point is the free car park at Rame Head,
SX421488. Several moderate ascents, but mostly easy walking.

From the beach and square at Cawsand, walk past the front of the
Cross Keys and up a narrow street, which will bring you to the village
car park. From the top of the car park, leave by the vehicle entrance
and turn left up the main road (not usually busy). After 350m turn
right (FORDER HILL) and immediately left (PUBLIC FOOTPATH). Climb
steadily to a lane, then turn right and keep climbing.

At the top, bear left on the PUBLIC FOOTPATH which is also the
access drive to Polhawn Fort (a wedding venue). Bear right on a footpath signed to Polhawn and Monk Rock Cottages. Ignore turnings on

4

The view from Rame Head

Kingsand, the twin village of Cawsand. At one time the Cornwall-Devon county boundary divided the two parts of the village. What united them was a deep involvement in the smuggling industry!

the right, then follow the coast path above the cottages and steeply up, crossing the access drive and climbing more steps.

Another 1km will bring you to Rame Head. When you arrive, you may want to walk out to the chapel perched on top. (Incidentally, the coastwatch station just inland by the car park has public toilets.)

Continue along the coastpath. When you reach a tarmac track making a horseshoe bend, take the right fork. Follow the track left at Penlee Point. When it forks, bear right on the gravel track.

The coastpath from here is waymarked, sometimes a footpath and sometimes using sections of access drives. Follow it back to the little square at the centre of Cawsand.

If you have time, it is well worth continuing up GARRETT STREET and following it round to Kingsand, which is even more picturesque.

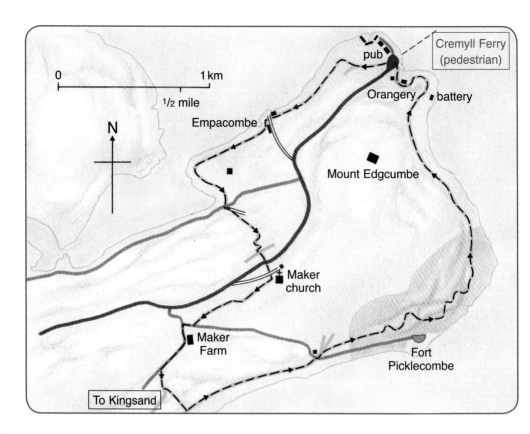

Walk 2 Cremyll Ferry and Maker

Distance: 8.4km (5¹/₄ miles)
Time: 2¹/₂ hours
*Character: A mixture of attractive farmland and the woods of the
Mount Edgcumbe Country Park. Mostly easy walking, but two steep
ascents and two steep descents.*

Start from the Cremyll pedestrian ferry. From the bus turning circle,
take PUBLIC FOOTPATH EMPACOMBE. Keep right at a junction.

At Empacombe, continue ahead to the little harbour (not into
Empacombe House), then walk on to the grass and turn left round the
grassy edge of the harbour wall to a stile.

The path first carries on in the same direction, then curves left.
Cross a lane onto PUBLIC FOOTPATH MAKER. After 30m, bear right off
the track on a well-beaten path up the slope. At the top of the field, go
through a kissing-gate and turn right. Turn left at the next junction
(yellow waymark).

Even with zig-zags it's a steep climb. Cross an unmarked track and climb five steps. Cross the road, PUBLIC FOOTPATH. Cross a drive, and at Maker church turn right, away from the church tower, keeping the edge of the field on your left, then after 100m cross a stile on the left. A waymarked path leads past Friary Manor Hotel to a lane.

Turn right along the lane and at a road junction turn left. Follow this lane till a lovely view opens up. Then bear left down a grassy track (PUBLIC FOOTPATH). After 90m turn left, PUBLIC FOOTPATH TO THE COAST PATH. (If you want to visit Kingsand, continue ahead here.)

There's a steep descent. On reaching the coast path, turn left. After 1km you will reach a lane. Turn right, then after 50m left (COAST PATH) through a gate. Take the path to the right, running alongside the lane, and follow coast path (acorn) waymarks through the Mount Edgcumbe Country Park.

Unfortunately a cliff fall has required a diversion involving rather a lot of steps, but ultimately you will rejoin the original route, which winds and undulates gently, with views of Plymouth and the Sound to your right, and later of the formal gardens to your left.

You will pass the Battery, then circle round to pass in front of the Orangery (refreshments). At the park entrance gate turn right, back to the ferry. You might find the Edgcumbe Arms a useful place to wait!

In the smuggling days, a visiting dean was taken to the top of Maker church tower to see the view – and was surprised to observe 20 casks of spirits lodged in the gutters!

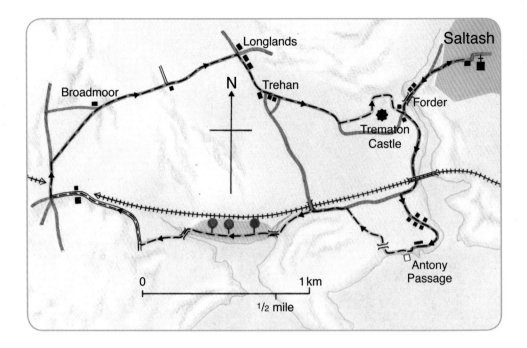

Walk 3 Trematon Castle and Antony Passage

Distance: 7.2km (4¹/₂ miles)
Time: 1³/₄ hours
Character: Lovely views of the Tamar, creeksides, fields and woodland on the way out; then quiet lanes and a view of the keep of Trematon Castle on the way back. Several moderate ascents.

Find roadside parking near St Stephen's church on the south-west edge of Saltash (SX417584). Walk westward down St Stephens Hill and cross Forder bridge.

Keep left along the lane (not the private track beside the creek) and follow it under the railway viaduct. At a junction, turn left. This lane will take you to the little harbour at Antony Passage.

Walk past the cottages and down to the beach. Turn right and walk behind a concrete platform, then turn right off the beach, and climb steps. The path runs along the cliff, then ducks right under a disused railway embankment.

Climb to a lane and turn left along it. When the lane turns right across the modern railway line, continue ahead (PUBLIC FOOTPATH).

This leads for 1.2km through a variety of pleasant scenery to a tarmac drive. Turn right, and follow it up to a road junction.

Turn right and after 230 m bear right, TREMATON FOR VEHICLES OVER 7'0". Keep right at a junction, then press on up to a crossroads.

Turn right, TREHAN TREMATON CASTLE. Continue ahead at the next two junctions. When you get your first view of the castle, opposite the entrance to Higher Castle Farm, bear left, PUBLIC FOOTPATH.

Follow the path down and left to a stile, then down an enclosed path. Turn right at the foot, and then left onto the lane, and retrace your steps up St Stephens Hill.

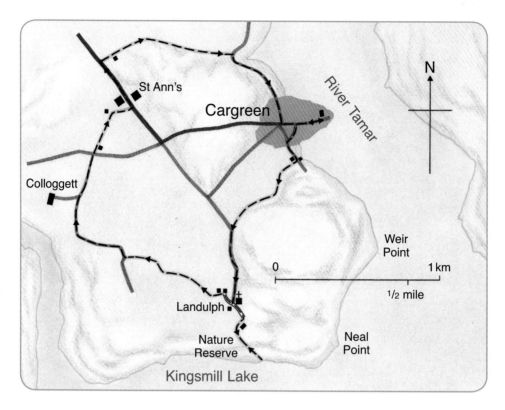

Walk 4 Cargreen and Landulph

Distance: 5.8km (3¹/₂ miles)
Time: 1¹/₂ hours
Character: Quiet footpaths and lanes, with two visits to the riverside, an ancient quay and ferry crossing at Cargreen, and a marsh nature reserve at Landulph. Easy walking.

Start at Landulph church, where there is roadside parking (SX 431615). At the foot of the lane, turn right, PUBLIC BRIDLEWAY.

Follow the bridleway for 1km, to a lane, and turn right. Ignore a lane on the left, then at a T-junction continue ahead on a track (PUBLIC FOOTPATH).

Enter a field and keep the hedge on your left to a stile, then continue with the hedge on your left across a second field. Leave by a stile and turn left along a slightly busier lane for 300m, past 'St Ann's' and 'Tamara'. Turn right (PUBLIC FOOTPATH) and keep the hedge on your right across two fields.

Then cross a large field. The direct line to the stile on the far side is

at about '2 o'clock' (100° or just south of due east if you have a com-
pass), but if the path has not been re-established try not to damage the
crop and go round the edge.

Continue across a second field in the same direction, go through a
kissing gate and turn right along a lane.

Although a footpath is shown on the OS map, and is signed along
the bank, it is passable only at low tide, and even then is slippery. (The
same applies to a footpath to Weir Point.) So continue along the lane
to a T-junction, and turn left down to the quay.

Then retrace your steps up as far as 'Tamar' (with a red phone box
in front at the time of writing). Turn left along a back street, keep left
at a junction and pass the village play area.

Immediately beyond 'Penyoke Barn' turn right (PUBLIC FOOTPATH).
This soon leads up a field to a stile: turn right along the field edge to
a gate and stile, then continue along the enclosed path to a lane. Turn
left, back to the church.

It is worth taking a further short stroll of 450 m each way. Turn left
at the bottom of the lane and follow a footpath out to a shingle beach,
passing a nature reserve with an explanatory notice board.

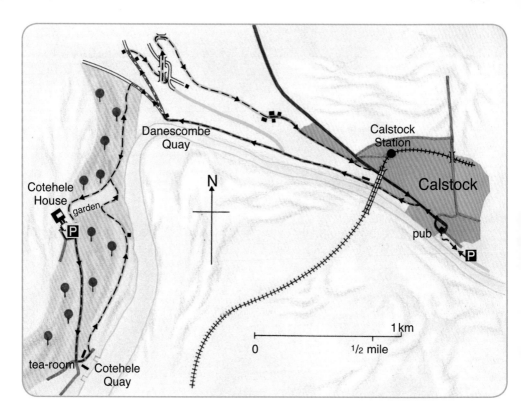

Walk 5 Calstock and Cotehele

Distance: 5.5km (3¹/₂ miles)
Time: 1¹/₄ hours, plus time at Cotehele
Character: From the attractive former river port of Calstock by way of the riverside lane and woodland paths to Cotehele House and gardens (National Trust) and Cotehele Quay (also National Trust but no entry fee), then on the return exploring the incline plane which once served the mining area above it. Several moderate ascents.

Start from the quayside car park in Calstock, walk along the river bank towards the viaduct. Turn inland behind the Tamar Inn and turn left into COMMERCIAL STREET.

After 50m bear left into a riverside lane which leads under the viaduct and past boatyards to Danescombe Quay, where it turns inland beside a creek and becomes a track. Pass a terrace of cottages and turn left on a footpath (COTEHELE HOUSE). The path climbs quite steeply. At a junction, continue ahead, climbing gently, with views of the gardens on your left.

12

Cross the front of the house, and then cross a courtyard, from which there is access to the house and/or gardens (entry fee). Leave by the gateway on the far side and turn left along the drive. After 100 m, turn left and immediately right, and walk downhill to the Quay, where you will find among other things a historic Tamar barge, the *Shamrock*, a Discovery Centre, and refreshments at the Edgcumbe Arms – now a tea-room rather than a pub.

Walk to the car park. Bear left on a path, which soon becomes a track leading along the valley bottom. Level at first, it then rises gently past a little chapel, then past the foot of the gardens and a viewpoint over the Tamar, to the junction you passed earlier. Keep right and right again, retracing your steps to the creekside track.

Turn right, then after 150 m turn sharp left, PUBLIC FOOTPATH. Climb till you pass a house, then after another 50 m turn sharp right up an unsigned path. This leads up to a footbridge. Pass under the bridge, then turn right and right again to cross it. You are now on the incline plane.

A path leads on over a second footbridge to an over-bridge. Turn left, then right to cross this bridge, and follow a footpath which eventually becomes a tarmac lane. Continue under the viaduct and back down to the quay.

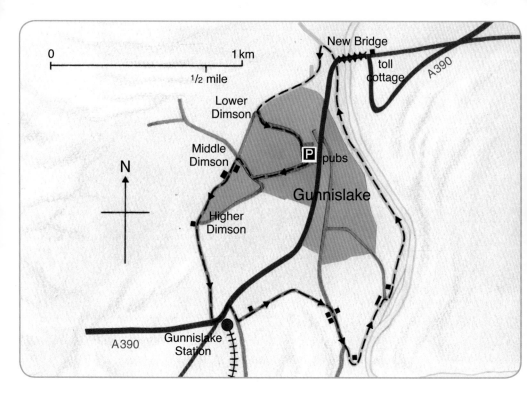

Walk 6 Gunnislake

Distance: 5.2km (3¹/₄ miles)
Time: 1¹/₂ hours
Character: Paths and quiet lanes around this 19th century industrial village, returned to woodland peace now that the mines and quarries have been abandoned. One steep ascent, one long steady ascent.

Start from the town centre car park or, even better, arrive by train and start from the station.

Turn right out of the station, and immediately right again into WELL PARK ROAD. After 50m turn left and descend STONY LANE to a T-junction. Turn right, and after 200m bear left (PUBLIC FOOTPATH).

Pass a house then follow the path to the left along the Tamar bank. (There was a short canal here to bypass a weir, which is why for a time the river is at a distance.) A few metres after the path becomes a track, turn right to pass to the right of a pair of cottages, and follow the path all the way to New Bridge, which was new around 1520 and until 1961 was the lowest bridge on the Tamar for road traffic.

Cross the modern road, which dates from around 1830, and take

the PUBLIC FOOTPATH opposite. At the first footpath junction, turn left and climb a track through woodland (see box below).

When you reach a road, turn left down KING STREET (unless you're in a hurry to get back to the station, in which case carry straight on) and follow the road round to the right to the car park.

The village centre has three pubs to choose from. A writer in 1901 described Gunnislake: 'with no architectural pretensions, it seems to have been designed in a nightmare, built in a whirlwind'. There's an element of truth in that, but personally I think it's really attractive! Return to the car park.

From the car park, turn right up CHAPEL STREET past the chapel and school. The street winds up to a cross-roads, by 'Armada House'. Turn left and follow the lane as it winds up to the main road. Turn left, back down to the station.

> The track you will climb, and the lane through Dimson, was the original route up from the bridge. In fact the first highway atlas of England and Wales (1675) shows this track as the main Post Road from Exeter to Truro, and so it remained until the late 18th century. Modern Gunnislake did not exist – even in 1809, the earliest OS one inch map does not show it – and the 'highway' passed through Dimson on its way to Callington.

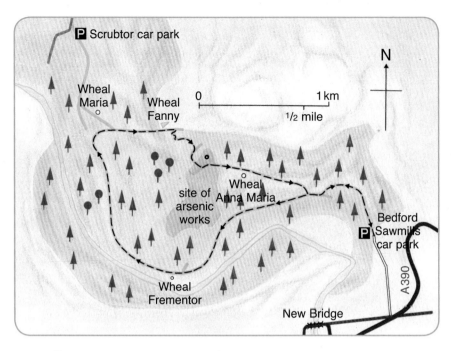

Walk 7 Devon Great Consols

Distance: 6km (3¾ miles)

Time: 2 hours

Character: This walk takes in the site of Europe's richest ever metal mine, but to be honest there is not a lot of industrial heritage interest for the non-specialist to see from the path – and away from the path there are hazards, so do not stray! Essentially this is a walk on broad tracks in superb woodland, predominantly coniferous.

Start from the Bedford Sawmills car park, signed off the A390 on the Devon side of New Bridge. Leave by the path at the far end of the car park. Ignore minor paths, and shouts of glee or terror from the adventure playground in the woods.

Keep left downhill at the first major junction, and keep left again at the next (WHEAL JOSIAH WALK). At the foot of the slope, keep right across the Blanchdown Adit.

At the next junction keep left, FREMENTOR MINE, and at the Wheal Frementor junction continue ahead, and pass a large hole – an 'open stope' is the technical term. Then pass through an area which is being managed for the benefit of the Heath fritillary butterfly.

After another kilometre, you will arrive at a junction marked as Point 3 (Wheal Fanny). You could make a diversion to the left, 400m

each way, to see the site of Wheal Maria. Otherwise, keep right and continue to a pond on the left. This was a reservoir for a water-wheel – water power was preferred to steam on most of these mines.

Then take the steep path which zig-zags up to the right. At a junction turn right (WHEAL JOSIAH), then left. At the next T-junction turn left, for a more typical post-mining scene, largely caused by arsenic contamination. Fork right, WHEAL JOSIAH WALK, passing the Wheal Anna Maria arsenic tailings.

Bear left at the next junction, HANGINGCLIFF WOOD, and retrace your steps to the car park – uphill all the way I'm afraid!

The William Morris connection

William Morris, the hero of the Arts and Crafts movement, was for a time a hereditary director of Devon Great Consols. In fact his father and two uncles between them held a third of the original shares, and became very rich as a result. Wheal Emma (not visited in this walk) was named after William Morris's mother.

In his activity with the company, which by then was producing arsenic, William Morris resolutely disregarded the safety of his workforce, as well as the environment. Subsequently his famous wallpapers used 'arsenic green' dyes, which released toxic gas if they became damp. The medical profession had been warning about this for the previous 50 years, but Morris remained in denial.

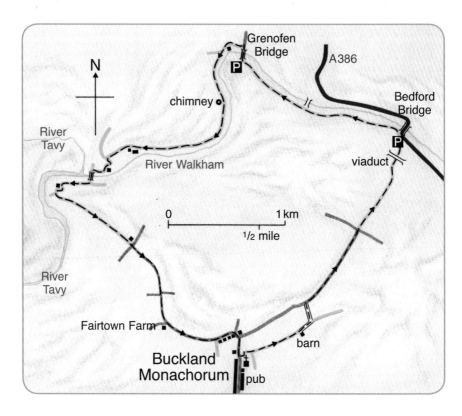

Walk 8   Bedford Bridge and Buckland Monachorum

Distance: 9km (5¹/2 miles)   Time: 2¹/2 hours
Character: Initially riverside woodland, then heathland and farmland,
with an attractive village (with pub) on the way. Several ascents and
descents, none particularly steep. Uneven walking in some places by
the river – and not to be attempted if the river is high.

Start from the car park immediately by Bedford Bridge, on the A386
Tavistock-Yelverton Road (SX 504703). From the car park entrance,
take the PUBLIC FOOTPATH heading north-west, which soon curves
round to follow the river bank.

Follow the bank for 1.5km, till you reach a stone bridge. Cross the
bridge, then turn left, PUBLIC BRIDLEWAY.

Keep left at a path junction. Follow the bridleway when it diverts
from the river, first passing through the remains of Westdown copper
mine, then diverting again to pass uphill of a house.

At a junction, turn left and zig-zag downhill. After another quiet
stretch of river, pass between two rocky outcrops and turn left.

18

Cross a footbridge, climb the bank, then turn right onto a track. This soon starts to climb, circling around a disused mine on the left – the Virtuous Lady Mine, said to be named after Queen Elizabeth I and first worked in 1558.

Keep left on the main track at the top. It climbs gently over a bracken-clad hillside, with views over Dartmoor and the Walkham valley. The track becomes a lane.

At a crossroads, continue ahead, BUCKLAND MONACHORUM, then keep left at Fairtown Farm. Entering the village, stay on the lane even when a footpath offers on the right. Keep right at a junction (CRAPSTONE), right again at the next, and walk as far as the church.

Take the PUBLIC FOOTPATH to the left, between the churchyard and Lady Modyford Hall. At a stile, continue ahead, through several fields and a barnyard. Follow the track when it turns left, and on reaching the lane turn right. Climb gently to a road junction.

Walk ahead in the same direction across the grazing common – look for an existing path in roughly the right direction rather than walking through the bracken. You will find yourself funnelled down into a valley. Cross a stream and pass under a railway viaduct. Further downhill, the path bears left back to the car park.

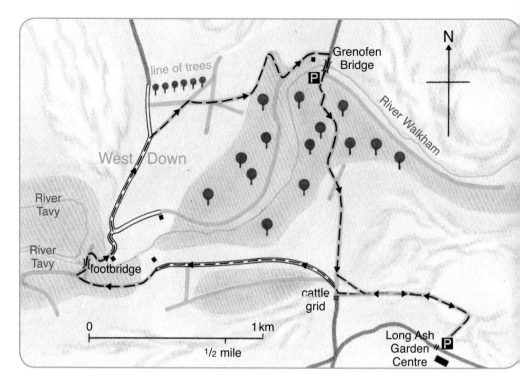

Walk 9 Long Ash and West Down

Distance: 7 km (4¹/₂ miles)
Time: 1³/₄ hours
Character: A mixture of grassy common pasture, bracken-covered moorland and lovely riverside woodland. Long ascents and descents, mostly gentle but with occasional steep sections.

Start from the parking area opposite Long Ash Garden Centre (SX 497694). To get there, from the A 386 at the southern end of Horrabridge take the turning signed CRAPSTONE BUCKLAND MON., then take the first turning right.

Walk away from the lane and garden centre, with a mature hedge on your left. After 200 m, turn left (WEST DEVON WAY) and follow the broad path, keeping left when in doubt.

At a parking/picnic area, turn right on a rough track which soon becomes tarmac, sweeping gently down into the valley. When the tarmac ends, continue ahead on the track till you arrive at a river, with a footbridge visible. This is the junction of the River Walkham with the River Tavy, known as Double Waters.

20

Walk a little beyond the footbridge, then turn right and head back to cross it. Follow the path ahead, but then turn right uphill to pass between rocks (see photo above) and down to join a riverside path through woodland. When it passes a house, it becomes an access track, and climbs quite steeply. Keep left at a junction and follow the track which now climbs steadily.

At a point just after a concrete gutter crosses the tarmac, bear right on a grassy path through the bracken towards a telephone pole. At a path crossing, bear right, then at the next crossing (by a stone wall with a hedge above it) continue ahead with the wall on your left.

The path swings left, runs along the top edge of a wood, then turns sharp right at a fingerpost, descending towards the river. At the foot, turn left along the river, then circle behind a house to reach a lane.

Turn right, cross the bridge, and continue ahead past the car park, up a rough track which becomes a 'holloway' – an old packhorse route etched into the landscape. It zig-zags upward.

When you emerge from the woodland, continue ahead through the bracken till you reach a bench, then bear diagonally left, to retrace your steps back to the car park.

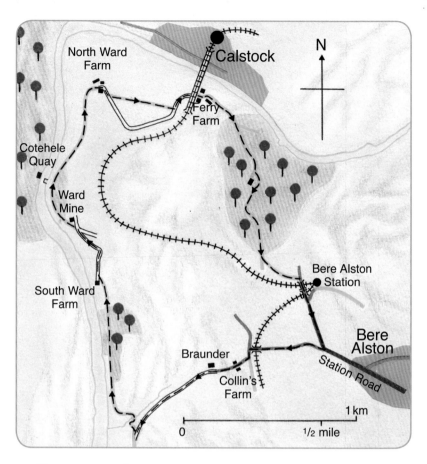

Walk 10   Bere Alston

Distance: 5.9km (3³/₄ miles) if starting from the station
Time: 1¹/₂ hours
Character: A very attractive walk through farmland and woodland,
with views of Cotehele Quay and the Calstock Viaduct. One long
steady ascent.

The best starting point is Bere Alston station. (You could start from
nearer the village. Entering by the B3257, bear right at the Edgcumbe
Hotel and find on-street parking in Station Road.)

Leave the station yard by the vehicle exit and turn left (VILLAGE
CENTRE). At a road junction, turn right (BRAUNDER HELSTONE).
Follow this lane down, cross the railway and turn left (BRAUNDER).
Ignore the footpath on the left. When the lane ends, continue ahead
(PUBLIC FOOTPATH) through the farmyard and down the main track.

When the track enters a field, a pedestrian gate 10m to the right is the waymarked footpath. Turn right and wind round to cross a stream. Turn left down the field with the hedge on your left, and then right along the bottom edge of the field.

After a short stretch of woodland, enter South Ward Farm, with views across the river. Pass the farmhouse and walk up its access drive.

At a track junction with a rather ambiguous fingerpost, turn left through a gate on the footpath through WARD MINE. A waymarked path leads into woodland, past a landing stage opposite Cotehele Quay, and then through fields to North Ward Farm.

Bear left on a rough track parallel to the river. (The fingerposts had been mischievously turned through 180° when I walked it last!) Reaching a lane, turn left to pass under the viaduct and into a farm-yard. Turn left, then right past cottages on a bankside path.

The path then bears right into woodland. Fork right at a junction and climb steadily. At the next junction keep left, and then forward at the junction after. Circle round the head of a small valley and climb again, to a stile. Keep left on the main path which leaves the wood and climbs through grassland to a lane. Turn right, under the bridges, then left to the station.

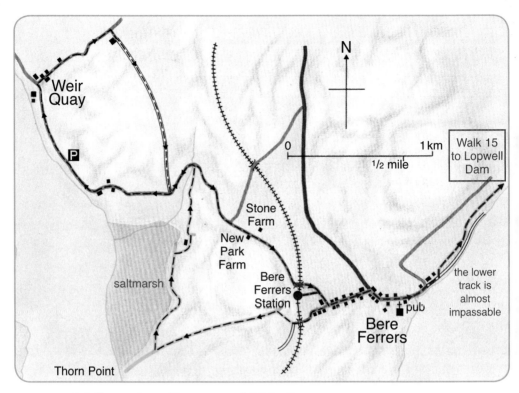

Walk 11   Bere Ferrers and Weir Quay

Distance: 8km (5 miles)
Time: 2 hours
Character: Initially field paths, with opportunities for birdwatching near the Tamar saltmarsh, but please don't trespass on the tidal foreshore. Then quiet lanes and tracks. The parking area indicated on the map south of Weir Quay is an alternative starting point.

Ideally start by taking the train to Bere Ferrers. Now this is a minor branch line, but once it was the main LSWR line from London to Plymouth. Coming out of the station, turn right. After 100m, turn right again (STATION ROAD, no through road). Beware: all three roads at this junction are called Station Road!

Cross under the railway then continue ahead on a rough track. Keep left at a junction, cross a stile and follow the path ahead, which climbs through two fields, then descends towards Thorn Point and the former ferry crossing to Cargreen.

At the foot of the third field, turn right (unless you want to make your way out to Thorn Point) and keep the lower edge of the field on

24

your left. At the end of the field, follow the hedge round then – after 100 m – turn left over a stile.

When you reach a junction, turn right (TAMAR VALLEY DISCOVERY TRAIL) – a brief diversion which avoids a marshy area as well as a property – and follow the waymarked path out to a lane. Turn left, and follow the lane up and then down, then along the riverside. Just past the Weir Quay boatyard, turn right up a lane (COTTS).

The lane climbs steadily to a road junction. Turn right here, along what soon becomes a rough track. When you reach a lane, turn left and follow it up the hill on the far side. At a junction continue ahead, BERE FERRERS, which will bring you back to the station.

Market gardening in the Tamar Valley

The sheltered conditions of the valley meant that it was able to produce the earliest daffodils and the earliest strawberries in Britain. From 1853 to the 1950s, as many as 10,000 people worked in the industry in the busiest months. Initially the produce was taken to Saltash Station for rapid shipment to London, then in 1890 the LSWR reached Bere Ferrers (itself a major fruit growing area) and the Cornish growers began to bring their produce to Cargreen. It was ferried across to Thorn Point, then up to the station by the track used in this walk.

Walk 12   Launceston and St Stephens

Distance: 5.5km (3 1/2 miles)
Time: About 1 1/2 hours
Character: Entirely a town walk. Launceston is probably the most interesting town in Cornwall: if it were in Tuscany, English tourists would make a bee-line for it, rather than rushing past on the A30 as they mostly do! The walk is in two parts: a very short walk around the town centre, then an exploration of the older settlement at St Stephens. One steep ascent, two steep descents.

The town centre

Start from the multi-storey car park in Westgate Street and walk past the Westgate Inn, then bear left to the town square. Notice the doorway of the White Hart Hotel: its stonework was recycled from an Augustinian Priory, founded in 1136. Keep right at the far end of the square, noticing the old bootmaker's sign above one of the shops.

Turn right into Southgate Street to take a look at the surviving town gateway. Seen from the other (outer) side, it made a grand entrance to the medieval walled town, and indeed to Cornwall, since many travellers arrived by way of Exeter Street, having crossed the Tamar at Polson Bridge.

Return along Southgate Street then continue ahead until you reach the church, St Mary Magdalene, which Nikolaus Pevsner described in *The Buildings of England* as 'the most spectacular church west of Exeter' though he says its amazing carved granite exterior is 'decorated with barbarous profuseness'. I fear he was giving marks for effort but not for style.

The church dates from around 1520. Before that, Launceston only had a chapel, its mother church being St Stephens across the valley. Don't miss the recumbent statue at the east end.

Carry on past the church and keep left down to a street of elegant Georgian houses, a reminder that the Assizes and other county town functions sometimes brought grand personages to Launceston, and Cornwall accommodated them in style. (One of these houses is the Lawrence House Museum, free entry and well worth a visit.)

Turn left, and enter the bailey of the castle, passing the remains of 'Lanson gaol', a dungeon of fearsome reputation. Leave by the main gate, and the car park is all too clearly visible ahead of you.

Above left: the view from St Stephen's Hill, with the castle dominating the town

Above right: the South Gate

Below right: the town square

Launceston's history

The castle is mentioned in Domesday Book (1087) so it must have been started very soon after the conquest in 1066, and reached its peak in the 13th century. It is maintained by English Heritage (much to the irritation of many Cornish people who regard it as part of *Cornish* heritage rather English) and it can be visited.

The old name of the settlement on the north side of the Kensey valley was Lan-Stephan, meaning 'churchyard of Stephen'. The Saxons made it Lan-Stephan-tun, and by corruption the later town on the south side (originally called Dunheved) is now variously pronounced 'Launston', 'Launs'n' or 'Laans'n'.

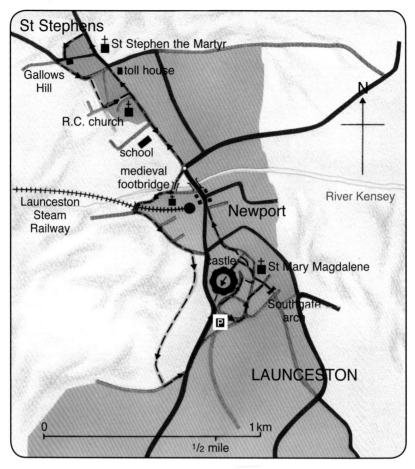

The longer walk

From the castle gateway, turn left and follow the wall up. Take a left turn into an unpromising back street. When it swings left, take a narrow alley to the right.

Turn left, and left again at the church, but this time, opposite the Methodist church, take a footpath which descends past the side of the employment office. In earlier times, when there were no wheeled vehicles in Cornwall, this was the main road.

Walk down, crossing two streets. On meeting a major road, cross with care to the pavement on the other side (and notice the narrow gauge Launceston Steam Railway below). Carry on past the traffic lights, over the River Kensey, and past the Gothick 'round house', with its explanatory plaque, to a mini-roundabout.

Continue up ST STEPHENS HILL, past very old cottages on the left.

Pass the toll house and cross over to take a look at the church. (There is an interesting Norman carving on the outside east wall.)

The Saxons built St Stephens to a grid-plan, which you can still just about discern if you look hard. Continue on the Bude road for another 100 m beyond the church, then turn left into NORTH STREET, which swings left and passes the front of the Golf Club. Turn right at the old elementary school, then left and left again at GALLOWS HILL – the traditional place of execution.

Immediately after 'Field End', turn right down a green lane (part of the Saxon grid-plan) as far as a street. The green lane continues down, but there is no through route, so turn left along the street. Walk ahead into HOLLIES CLOSE and take the footway at the far end out to St Stephens Hill. Turn right, and return to the mini-roundabout.

Keep right along WESTBRIDGE ROAD and cross the river by a medieval footbridge leading to St Thomas's church. Behind the church once stood an Augustinian priory, of which very little remains.

Turn right at the church and follow the curving lane to cross the railway. Turn left at the T-junction.

Pass a terrace of cottages, then continue ahead at the junction. Follow a track to the right of FOUNDRY GARDENS. Pass two more terraces then turn right on PUBLIC FOOTPATH. Follow the waymarked path, with its views of the castle towering above you.

On reaching a lane, turn left and climb to join the main road. Continue as far as the castle gate, then turn right to the car park.

Some suggestions for there-and-back walks

Walk 13   Luckett

You can walk in either direction from the (free) car park in Luckett, which is best approached from the southerly (Kit Hill) direction.

Turn left out of the vehicle entrance of the car park and the lane takes you to Greenscombe Wood, a nature reserve. You can either follow the waymarked Tamar Valley Discovery Trail, or use the permissive paths in the woodland as indicated on notice boards.

In the opposite direction, a waymarked path leads to Horsebridge, slightly under 2 km (1 1/4 miles), where you will find 'The Royal Inn and Horsebridge Brewery' (01822 870214).

Turn right out of the pedestrian entrance to the car park, then right again (PUBLIC FOOTPATH). The track leads to a gate. Turn left and keep the hedge on your left. At the end of the field, turn left to cross a stile, then a simple footbridge. Enter a field and keep the hedge on your right and leave by the metal gate at the far end. Turn right along a drive, go through the farmyard and continue on a rough track which leads to the bridge, which was built in 1437.

Walk 14   Tavistock Canal

Just about unique in Devon, this is a lovely walk of 4 km each way which is entirely flat! Start westward from Tavistock following the riverside path through the park, then bear right to the underpass at the far end. Once through the underpass, turn right up the steps and left along the canal towpath.

It takes a little time to escape fully from the town, but then the walk gets better and better. Highlights are Crowndale, birthplace of Francis Drake, and the Shillamill railway viaduct. Another 800 m further on, you can follow the canal over the 18 m high Lumburn aqueduct – but after that the towpath is blocked, because the canal disappears into a tunnel.

Walk 15   Bere Ferrers Station to Lopwell Dam

See map on page 24. A very pleasant walk, 2.8 km (1 3/4 miles) each way. You can alternatively start from Lopwell, where there is a car park east of the River Tavy (SX 475649) but beware: the narrow path across the dam is totally submerged for several hours at high tide, so time your walk carefully to avoid being marooned!

From Bere Ferrers station, turn right. After 100 m keep left at the T-junction, then at the next T-junction turn right. Pass 'The Olde Plough Inn' and the quay. When the lane turns inland, continue ahead on a creekside track. After 200 m, just beyond an old barn, bear left at a waymarked stile. (The main track is virtually impassable mud.) At a path junction, keep left on a footpath which leads to a lane.

Turn right along the lane, which swings right across a creek then left at a junction. Climb steeply. Opposite a corrugated iron barn, turn right down a rough track, which soon swings left and descends the valley side to Lopwell Dam.

Above: the Tavistock Canal

Right: Lopwell Dam, behind which is a reservoir, now disused

Some other Bossiney walks books

Shortish walks – Bodmin Moor
Shortish walks near the Land's End
Shortish walks on and around The Lizard
Shortish walks in north Cornwall
Shortish walks – St Ives to Padstow
Shortish walks – Truro to Looe

Shortish walks on Dartmoor
Really short walks – North Dartmoor
Really short walks – South Dartmoor
North Dartmoor pub walks
South Dartmoor .ub walks
Walks on High Dartmoor

Shortish walks – The South Devon Coast
Shortish walks – Torbay and Dartmouth
Really Short Walks – South Devon

We publish walks books covering Devon, Cornwall and Somerset.
For a full list, please see our website, www.bossineybooks.com